Relationships Open Doors

Putting clients and their needs first
can be the best thing you'll ever do
for your company's business.

James P. Naughton

KEY
Publishing Company

Relationships Open Doors
by James P. Naughton

ISBN 978-0-9858377-2-3

© 2015 by James P. Naughton
Key Publishing Company

JP Naughton Sales Performance Company

www.KeysForSellingSuccess.com

Facebook

Printed in the United States of America

Editing, layout, design and cover by
Kip Williams for Print-Ink Press©
mrkipw@gmail.com

Author picture on back cover:
Soozie Sundlun of East Greenwich Photo & Studio
(www.egphoto.com, www.egphotoweddings.com)

Looking to increase your sales? The following is intended to provide a window for you to peer into and learn from *forty years in sales career(s) of someone who has through trial and error, "done it all and done it very successfully." Instead of suggesting a series of steps to take, the author brings you along for the ride.*

Book Dedication

I dedicate this book to my close friend, mentor and former boss K.David Millbury.

Dave and I first met in 1981, and we quickly became friends. Although we were employed by different companies, he became my teacher and coach during the transition into my new Wall Street sales career. After turning down a couple of his early offers of employment, (which he has never let me forget), I finally accepted and began working for him in 1987. As I mention in my first book, *Jump In and Start Swimming*, I learned more about the business, selling and relationship building, and earned more money, and had more fun and laughs along the way, than I ever dreamed possible. We stay in touch and continue to have some laughs a couple times a week. I can only hope that you will be as fortunate to find a mentor like Dave for you career.

From one Marine to another Dave, *Semper Fi!*

Foreword

I have spent over 40 great years in various sales and wholesaling careers. In fact, selling is the only occupation I have held since graduating college in 1971, and it has allowed me success beyond my wildest dreams. My first book, *Jump In and Start Swimming*, published in 2012, includes some general discussion regarding my sales accomplishments, however, at the request of my readers, I decided to get a little more specific and provide more details on the techniques which I employed to reach record setting sales goals.

Jump In and Start Swimming, in addition to providing an inside look into a unique and lucrative sales career, also includes examples of overcoming life and business obstacles. The title is a synonym for having faith in yourself and/or taking a "leap of faith." It also relates to thinking "outside the box," and listening to your intuition when it's telling you to try something new. A wise woman once told me that "playing it safe will not always create the desired progress you are looking for."

It was written partially at the request of a friend and CEO, who was also a college adjunct professor, looking for me to speak to his class on my career experiences after the stock market crash of 2008 and the subsequent recession. Layoffs began to hit all-time highs in '09 and it was beginning to resemble the Great Depression. College seniors and recent grads were finding it difficult, if not impossible, to obtain jobs and many of their parents were out of work, unable to pay student loans. So I kept writing, way beyond the college talk I was asked to prepare. I believed if I could help just a few students find their way and acquire a job it would be worth it. As a result two years later I published my first book, *Jump In and Start Swimming*, followed by a supplemental guide: *Job and Career Assistance for College Seniors and Recent Grads*, which provides a number of pointers to help one get a job.

My father landed on Ellis Island in the fiercely cold winter of 1930 with "the shirt on his back" and spent about six months in a bread line in the Battery section of Manhattan before finding work as a laborer. Growing up, I listened to his stories of the era, regarding how folks survived or didn't, without Unemployment Insurance, Social Security, Medicare… i.e., without anything. I kept writing because in addition to my friend's request for a copy of my proposed talk to his business class, I also thought that the obstacles my father and family faced and surmounted during the depression years, along with the jobs and careers I found before and after college, might be of help, not only to my friend's college class, but also to anyone looking for a job and struggling within what I refer to as the Second Great Depression. Later, in response to my readers' emails, as previously mentioned, I published a supplemental guide for *Job and Career Assistance for College Seniors and Recent Grads* which I offer free to purchasers of a paperback copy. (It is also available by itself for $1.99 on Amazon/Kindle, Barnes & Noble/Nook) In the guide I list some government statistics that show the annual salaries of many various careers. When I first glanced at them, I realized how fortunate I was to have chosen a career in sales. There was not a single career that offered anywhere near the earnings available to good sales people.

I began my sales career after graduating college in the 70s. Thirty years later, I was selling close to One Billion Dollars in a single year (actually it was $10 million short, but as author Richard Carlson, states in his book, "Don't Sweat the Small Stuff"). Hopefully it will become apparent to my readers that my use of large sales numbers, while true, doesn't actually correlate with what I earned, which was measured in basis points. A real estate sales person can receive up to six percent on the sale of house, so if they sell a million (could be from just one house sale), that's $60,000 in commissions. Multiply that by any number of house sales in a good year and one could envision earning a very good annual income on a few million dollars off real estate sales vs. a billion dollars of financial product sales. In other words a billion sounds like a lot and it is, but I use it as an "attention getter" to attract readers. If we base success on how much money one earns, one could be deemed more successful in another sales career while selling significantly less in product. This book is designed to provide you with insight into becoming the best sales person you can. The money-earnings will follow, regardless of what type of sales you choose. And while making a good living is considered part of one's success, it's just that: "part of it."

As an aside, I should mention that my childhood wasn't easy and I didn't do well in high school; I almost dropped out completely if it wasn't for that one particular teacher who cared and try to help. [We just reunited after 40+ years. A former high school classmate who attended my recent book signing did a search and found that he is a Professor of English at Quinnipiac University: Professor Leonard Engel. The sight of us meeting and exchanging books was surreal.] I did graduate, however, I received 704 on my SATs (total), so college seemed out of the question, and at the time I didn't much care. After a short stint in the Marines I became an electric power lineman. I wasn't the brightest bulb on block (no pun intended), but I didn't have a fear of heights, and the money was great.

Tragically one of our field managers got electrocuted and died horribly. Later, I became seriously ill with mononucleosis. Both events brought about a change of direction in my life.

I started thinking about school. I tried Ward School of Electronics in the evening but couldn't keep up with the math. Next, I took some courses at a local college and did reasonably well. An instructor mentioned a term that I had never heard of: "matriculation"; he said if I continued to do well, that I could switch, i.e. matriculate, into college full time, regardless of the low SAT scores. I ended up doing exactly that and graduated with a Liberal Arts degree with a major in English.

Table of Contents

Dedication v

Foreword vii

A Brief Overview of my Selling Careers 1

I   More Building and Maintaining 9

II   Why People Buy From You 15

III   My Selling and Wholesaling Experiences 21

IV   Trust, Friendship and Showing Up 27

V   Empathy, Sincerity, and Service 31

VI   Marketing and Selling 37

VII   Selling with Stories 41

VIII   Competition 47

IX   "Flash in the Pan" 49

X   Group Presentations: Seminars, Conventions 53

Author's Thoughts on Success 59

A Brief Overview
of the Author's Selling Careers

I was hired into the business world after
college by the Travelers Insurance Company,
and attended their insurance school for a year.
(Unfortunately for today's graduates, very few,
if any, companies provide that kind of training.)
After completing my training, I was assigned to
the Princeton, New Jersey, field office as a Group
Insurance Account Executive. My primary respon-
sibility was to sell Group Insurance Products by
creating and maintaining "relationships" with
insurance brokers such as Johnson Higgins and
Marsh McLennan. In that era, my training had a
heavy emphasis on insurance product knowledge;
the sales training was handled on the job in the
"field." Also, the maintaining of existing relationships and establishing new relationships were really not taught or discussed as they might be today.
They were also left up to "on-the-job" training.
In any event, the concept of relationship building
began to slowly sink in subliminally.

Due to the fact that I was selling employee
benefits, I was often requested to be at the point of
sale by the broker which made him RELY ON MY

EXPERTISE. After a few sales, this made me VALU-ABLE to his business which in return GAINED HIS TRUST, thus turning him from a customer to a relationship. As previously mentioned, while I knew that my efforts were paying off and were being noticed by management, the full understanding, perspective and importance of relationship building was still a ways off. In other words I was doing it almost from instinct in the beginning.

After a while he (the insurance broker) became comfortable with me servicing his client, possibly a medium size corporation. When the Human Resource department responsible for employee benefits needed a question or problem resolved, they began calling and relying on me as their main contact with my home office in Hartford, Connecticut. I would often give updates to employees at lunch meetings that the client would organize, allowing me to begin to create a relationship with the corporation while allowing the broker more time to obtain more prospects and customers. When a vice president of the Human Resource department moved to a new company, he called me for help with his new company's group insurance plan, and in turn I brought in the broker that had the group contract from his old firm. The broker began utilizing me to help build his business which meant more business for me. This is a beginning example of how important Relationship Building could be to your sales career.

While living near Princeton, I also sold men's and boy's clothes various times in the evening and

Saturdays. This part-time sales position provided me with a different set of challenges, as every sales job and product has unique characteristics which I will discuss later on. After a few years my entrepreneurial spirit compelled me to become an independent all-lines insurance agent selling every type of insurance product that existed including annuities. During this time, I attended a month-long property casualty school for personal and also commercial lines of insurance. Later on, I was hired by a major insurance company to teach insurance product knowledge along with a selling skills course for rookie agents, mostly in a classroom setting and occasionally in the "field." I was fortunate to have had the opportunity to learn from a variety of insurance and sales consultants to help build training programs for the agents. Due to extensive phone sales techniques I learned from experts brought in from the New England Telephone Company, I was asked to co-manage an evening telemarketing sales organization for our state newspaper which won first prize for bringing in the most new subscriptions in the US, beating out approximately 10,000 competitors (a lot different than how it was done in my early childhood years as a paper boy, when I alone was expected to bring in new customers for the former *Hartford Times*). All of these different types of sales jobs including telemarketing (sales via phone) had one thing in common. I needed to use the very basic selling process: getting attention, learning the potential customer's (prospect's) needs and/or problems to be solved, using open-ended and probing questions; then I would discuss how my products could fit their needs and finally I would close the sale (getting the order) in all of my attempts to sell something. Once you have mastered the basics then depending on what type of sales career you decide on, you will need to learn more advanced methods (i.e. like building relationships, consultative selling and asking for referrals) to sell as much of your company's products as possible. As stated in the books title, "Relationship Building" will be this book's core topic.

Next, I was hired by a major Wall Street stock brokerage firm to teach their advisors to sell Insurance/ Annuity products and accompany them at the point of sale. By the end of my first year I took my territory from the bottom 14th ranking to number one, and kept it there for the rest of my tenure.

Finally I accepted a position as a Regional Sales Vice President for a major mutual fund company where I was employed for 21 years until retirement. During all of my sales careers, I managed to rank in the in the top sales tier every year. In my last position I was a sales leader for 20 out of 21 years and was often number one not only in my firm but occasionally for the whole industry. If you personally knew me, you would know that I am basically a modest person and as a first generation American, I come from humble beginnings. So when I tell you about my success, it's not out of bragging but rather to get your attention (the 1st step in the basic sales process) and to show you that I might actually know something about sales and success.

I will only discuss techniques that I actually employed during my career(s) and it's my belief that my techniques were/are universal and can be employed in any type of sales career you choose. I should also point out that while most of these ideas come from my personal experience, some are also derived from books, tapes and other top salesmen and women which I might have internalized. Someone once said, "There is no such thing as a new sales idea." I can't say if that is true or not. However, I want you to know that whatever I learned, I worked EXTREMELY HARD to put it to great USE in my careers. This book is not about what I think you should do, but rather it's a description of one of the many disciplines, RELATIONSHIP BUILDING that I used to sell billions of dollars of products.

For those of you presently looking for a career in sales, if possible, get with someone or some company that has a good training program, hopefully some classroom-style training for the basics, followed by "hands on" in the field, during advanced training. You will need to practice opening a sales conversation — Attention Phase. In addition you will need to learn to ask probing questions specifically with your product in mind to uncover the prospect's real needs. And then you must show them how the features of your product will solve their problem and fill their needs. Finally, handling the reason you're there in the first place, i.e., learning how to close the sale. "Get an order." Some trainers will suggest that you should be "closing" all during the sales call. I never was able to do that because when starting out in my own sales career, I realized that some prospects, clients and relationships felt that I was being "pushy" and told me so. In fact a little later on, I will tell you more about the aforementioned part-time sales job that I had selling men's and boy's clothes in regards to my thoughts on relationship selling. For now, I will just tell you that in one year, I was selling more that any part-time and some full-time store salesmen. Unfortunately, I got fired, for amongst other things "being pushy" with the costumers and alienating many of the store's salesmen. So much for being "Numero Uno." It was a great lesson for me early on.

I also discovered early on in my career that sometimes a prospect just doesn't like, want or need your product. This might be referred to as REJECTION, meaning you take it personally. It's a sales term and fact of life that anyone in a sales career will have to deal with. How you let "no" AFFECT you and your getting future sales is key to your success in sales. It's human to feel a little down over the loss of a sale or a relationship. It's only damaging when you have received so many "no"s that it affects your work ethic. It's an important topic for sales training, however, I will not spend a lot of time on it in this book, other than to say, that early in my career, I personally had rejection problems and it really affected me. I was fortunate to have mentors who taught me how to handle it. The obvious way to deal with rejection is to get more "yes"s, i.e., more sales, which is a goal of this book on learning the art of relationship building. A well-known sales trainer I met in the early 90s, Bill Good, would tell us, "just continue looking for the cherries while throwing away the pits"; the more you throw away the closer you are to a cherry who will buy your product. It's probably not exact; I believe it's close and I think you get the picture. This book assumes that you have made reasonable progress in your sales career and have acquired a number of clients. You are now are ready to begin your ascent to the top sales position in your firm.

Chapter I
More Building and Maintaining

In my book *Jump In and Start Swimming,* I credit a great deal of my selling success on my ability to build and maintain relationships. While I realize that much has already been written lately on the subject, I have been encouraged by my readers to throw in my "two cents" on the subject. The reason I received so many requests to say more about the subject is due to the fact that I have shown by example, by my sales numbers, that my ideas have been proven to work. My experience is real and not a theory.

As previously mentioned, I first began building and maintaining relationships during my Group Insurance sales position, however, as I also mentioned, I was so busy "just doing and just learning" that I didn't have the time to analyze what methods were making me successful, till later on in my career. Hopefully, in discussing my methods, I will save you some time on your path to selling success.

Specifically, I am going to provide you with some powerful insight into the relationship building piece of the sales process, a skill that I learned and excelled at.

I should point out as we begin, that relationship building and consultative selling go hand and hand. Consultative selling requires a salesman to dig down deeper (referred to in sales lingo as *probing**) and learn as much detail about a customer, his business and his needs as you can. You are in effect engaging your prospect in a give-and-take conversation. In doing so, the information you uncover will allow you to better tailor your sales presentations to their needs and eventually over time enable you to turn the customer into a relationship. Listening to clients' needs takes practice, as beginning salespeople are often so eager to get the order, they try to close before they fully understand what the client actually needs. Good listening skills are not only part of the sales process but are very important in relationship building. Without listening skills how can one "relate" to another?

My first "ah-ha!" moment with regard to the value of relationships came early on in my Wall Street career, when one of my financial advisors in upstate New York, who was selling a huge amount of my annuity and insurance products, called a manager friend of his in Pennsylvania and told him all about how we were bringing in so much business doing public seminars together. He suggested

---

* Probing is a combination of open-ended questions combined with sincere listening which will take practice by a new sales person.

that the Pennsylvania Manager should consider setting up one of my seminars for his branch advisors and their clients. Sure, I could have called and asked the manager myself, but it carried a lot more weight coming from a very large, successful advisor. As you might have read in my first book, *Jump In and Start Swimming*, the manager not only thought it was worth the try, he took out a large ad in the main city newspaper, in addition to mailing a number of his branch clients. The response was terrific and we ended up with 300 attendees, many of whom opted to purchase my products. (I have a picture of the event that the local newspaper took the "night of" in my first book and I also received the first of many promotions to come because of that event.) I had spent a lot of time gaining the support and trust of the New York advisor: dropping by his office often, always bringing ideas of "what was working." I invited him and his wife to dinner. I got to know him, his wife, and an inside understanding of his business, including his product needs. I always offered to sponsor one of his seminars when I came into town, which was monthly. In fact, for one lunch seminar, I actually chartered a small plane to get me into town when my US Air flight was canceled. I am not suggesting you do everything I have done, but rather file this under, "do all that you can for your relationships." I did this at the spur of the moment, not knowing if my company would reimburse me. Luckily, they realized the benefit and did. The point is, in the beginning, while I might not have thought, "relationship," consciously, I definitely knew the value of this advisor as a relationship and was willing to incur a significant personal expense with the charter plane. This "ah-ha!" moment changed everything for the positive. This particular relationship example took approximately nine months to evolve, and continued for years. During this time I routinely brought him articles and other valuable information pertinent to his business. The Computer and Internet will allow you more opportunities to locate this kind of pertinent information. At this early time in my career, the computer was not available; in fact, when I had to make a simple phone call I often had to find a pay phone on the side of the road and I knew their whereabouts from here to Buffalo, a situation you will not have to deal with.

It's hard now to even consider how we operated with the communications of the 70s and 80s. My first cell phone, a Panasonic ($2500) was installed in 1989 with a transformer in the trunk; it could be used as a portable only in certain areas. When you took it outside the car it was approximately the size of a shoebox. I called often and mailed any items that I thought would be of help to him. I did everything possible to have him begin to RELY ON ME, not just for my products but as an EXPERT and a CONSULTANT to his practice. Suffice it to say, "Building relationships will take both time and a lot of effort." [I will discuss my experience presenting at group meetings, public and private client seminars that helped build my relationship with the New York advisor and others mentioned above later in Chapter X, "Group Sales Presentations." I will also include a discussion of your possible invitation to present at corporate clients conventions.]

The advisor not only became a strong relationship for my sales efforts, he became what I refer to as a "center of influence," meaning that in addition to repeat sales, he was recommending and introducing me to others like himself, i.e., referrals. In addition, he provided me "the lay of the land," i.e., what was happening in his branch and region, which enabled me to more easily navigate this part of my territory. He also became a friend and is still one today. I soon realized that I was in the preliminary stages of having others refer me and my products. I ended up with a lot of "clients" — customers who bought at least one of my products, however, turning them into relationships began to "skyrocket" my sales. As I mentioned earlier, learning to build relationships enabled me by the end of my first year to bring my territory from 14th place — the bottom — to number one, and it stayed number one for the next five years, until I accepted an offer to join another firm with more opportunities.

TAKE-AWAY NOTES
Foreword through Chapter I

• Master the selling basics open, probing, showing how the features of your product benefit the client, and closing and obtaining the order, then work on building relationships.

• "Rely On My/Your Expertise, with Service and Knowledge.

• Make yourself Valuable to Gain his Trust." Make yourself an EXPERT, not only for your product, but for your client and his business.

• Begin/learn to PROBE more deeply, called Consultative selling, become a great LISTENER, get REFERRALS.

• Get help early on in your career in dealing with REJECTION; WORK EXTREMELY HARD!

Chapter II
Why People Buy from You
(Assuming They Have a Need)

My new territorial Senior Vice President was an accomplished salesman who was exceptionally aware of the value of relationships and relationship selling. I can still recall him saying that, "there are three reasons people do business with you," then after a short pause he would rattle them off as follows:

1. "Because they LIKE you!"
2. "Because they LIKE you!" and
3. "Because they LIKE you!"

As a result of my forty years of sales experiences I know that his word "like" was intertwined with trust. People like you for a number of reasons, and trust is number one in building relationships. Why do people trust you? Because you KNOW YOUR PRODUCT and you are HONEST with them. You also provide excellent service to them. If not, you might get a sale, but that's it. "One." Forget about REPEAT SALES: they are not going to happen.

When sales were going through the ceiling, everyone loved the cliché, and when sales went in the tank, they did a 360° and felt the sales staff were relying too much on relationships and not asking for the order, i.e., not closing hard enough. My concern from a management perspective would be whether enough new relationships were being built to meet sales goals, particularly in the unlikely event that existing clients stopped buying because your product has ceased being competitive or due to malfunctions of your company's current product line. In other words, in my view, "relying on your relationships is never a problem; the problem is not building enough of them."

Suffice it to say that you never have enough relationships. Keep in mind that, while your main task is selling your product, you must be mindful of not alienating senior management regardless of whether you feel they grasp the sales process or not. So, you and sales management are in effect selling the company that you know what you are doing. At the risk of sounding flip, one way is to do this is to increase sales, and then gently give positive feedback on obstacles beyond your control, such as better products, reduced prices, and better performance of and by competitors, as well as changes in customer's habits thinking. You should provide this feedback to your sales manager not as an excuse, but with a marketing aspect to it. (Don't just tear things down, show ways to build them up!)Consider incorporating positives with your own products with any such feedback.

Just how important are relationships to your career? In the appendix of *Jump In and Start Swimming*, I quote statistics that the John Asher

Sales Consulting Firm researched on relationship selling. Here are a few pointers that I included in page 85 of the book: "Eighty percent of Business to Business (B2B) transactions are the result of relationship/consultative[†] type sales, where the buyer has to LIKE, TRUST, and get along with the seller." Asher goes on to say that "statistics tell the story": "Selling yourself is the most important sale in 80% of B2B sales."

Of course all of the above assumes your prospects, clients, relationships have a NEED that your product can truly fill and your ability to answer the client's ultimate question, "What's in it for me?" You should also be aware that when I speak of the power of relationships, I generally assume that all things are equal and that your product is as at least as good as the competition's (I found I could almost always uncover a feature or two of my product that was better than my competition's, even in the most competitive circumstances). Of course you will find out this isn't always the case. If the competition has much higher returns or more bells and whistles, i.e., a better product, having a great relationship won't guarantee you a sale, but it increases your odds as shown in the Asher report above.

I learned to think of it in this manner: building

† Consultative selling is a method of probing even deeper to better understand their needs and problems thus allowing you to better position the salient features of your product, and yourself as an expert. You are not only building, but you are cementing your relationship with them.

relationships are as important to sales, as building a strong foundation for a five- or ten-story office building, You still need to get those relationships to buy your products and you need to maintain them with great service. Likewise, once the building is complete, the owners are going to have to fill it with tenants and find ways to keep them happy! Selling to "clients" will allow you to keep your job, creating relationships will make you Number One and wealthy!

OK. So you have begun to build your relationships. How did they go from a purchaser of your product to an actual relationship?

I am going to assume that you employed a consultative sales process mentioned earlier, meaning that you have thoroughly profiled the potential buyer of your products. You have probed strategically and deeply over time with some open-ended questions ("What are your expectations for this product?" = open-ended; vs. "Do you see a need for this product?" = closed-ended) and found out some personal information including possibly his/her hobbies, golf, tennis, and marital situation if appropriate. Of course you learned as much about his/her business and their clients regarding what product he is carrying or has purchased in the past, and why. What would make his current product line even better? e.g., Price? Extra features? If you're selling to a vendor (such as a financial advisor or a store owner), ascertain whether his firm will allow him to sell your products.

TAKE-AWAY NOTES
Chapter II

• Selling yourself, getting clients to like you via TRUST.

• Know your product and be HONEST with your clients.

• YOU NEVER HAVE ENOUGH RELATIONSHIPS.

• Learn DEEP PROBING with CONSULTATIVE SELLING.

• Relationships equal Repeat sales and often better Referrals.

• Learn to provide management with field intelligence.

Chapter III
Some Thoughts on My Various
Selling and Wholesaling Experiences.

I discussed that, during my forty years in various sales careers, I sold men/boys clothing, and also insurance by cold calling door to door. I also managed a successful telemarketing sales program and taught a selling skills program in a classroom and in the "field" for a major US company. I also stated that "after graduating college, I became a group insurance sales representative, where I generally sold group insurance to corporations alongside of an insurance broker." In that situation, my first sale was selling myself, then my products and my company, to an insurance broker, and quite often I would accompany the broker on a sales call with his client. By offering to be at the point of sale, I pointed out that in effect I was building relationships with insurance brokers. Later on, as I also mentioned I sold financial products to financial advisors formerly known as stock brokers who in turn sold these products to their clients. I was considered a wholesaler, however, whenever folks asked me what I did for work, I proudly replied with "I am a salesman." Meaning whether selling direct or wholesaling, the basics are similar. With

21

wholesaling you're selling to someone who in turn will be selling your product to his clients, so you need to be selling from the perspective of where and how would this product fit with his clients. As you build relationships, you will know ahead of time how your product would solve some of his client's needs. If he is a financial planner you will have profiled him, and discovered things such as, "is he mainly equity oriented or does he do a lot of fixed income, etc.?" If you're selling IT Technology products, when your company unveils a new "breakthrough" software, you will already know who to call first.

Throughout my career, the sales basics were always the same in any type of sales or wholesaling, including the Attention phase: meeting with the client, learning about the client and uncovering his/her needs then discussing the features of your product and showing/demonstrating how they fill clients' needs and the Close, known as obtaining an order. These sales basics were/are the initial process for any sale.

When I was selling suits at Easter time to a man and his 10- and 12-year-old sons, the basic sales process was the same, but the pace of it was much quicker. Just as when I was selling life insurance door to door, I didn't have a lot of time to profile and probe the potential customer. I had to assume a "close" meaning that my brain registered, e.g., "young couple with a new baby." Often in door-to-door selling, I had to, in 5 minutes, help them realize that as difficult it might be for them to afford spending dollars on insurance premium at the moment, I would ask them to picture "how much harder it would be if something should happen to either one of the parents without having insurance, i.e., pointing out their NEED to protect their family. If you are wondering, door-to-door retail cold calling was not only difficult, but it was mentally and physically draining. It was not conducive to consultative selling from my perspective. Thinking back, "the positive part of this experience for me, was that it was like swinging 3 bats, meaning that when I was developing leads and setting appointments and creating relationships, it made the sales process seem so much easier and fun... not to mention the commissions that started pouring in." These door-to-door prospects were often "one sale" customers, meaning they seldom allowed for a repeat sale. Some eventually turned into relationships, however, without the time to employ a consultative-type sale approach, i.e., probing, questioning, or the ability to gain trust over time, relationships were more difficult and timely to develop. You can begin to see how Consultative Selling and Relationship Building go hand and hand.

As a men's/boy's clothing salesman, when I did sell a couple of suits to the father for his two sons, I made sure he had my card and would feel comfortable calling me if the suit need extra alterations etc., and I always had something for the kids, such as a pass for an ice cream cone at the nearby store. And finally I got permission to personally call him anytime we were going to be having a sale. With regards to selling life insurance door to door, if I did get a sale, unfortunately it wasn't too often. [You're correct if you're thinking, "he wasn't number one at everything." You're right! I admit it.]

I did get a little better when I decided to use a different close. I called it "Get an appointment close." Instead of following my sales manager's directive to make a quick close and get an immediate sale, I made my main goal to set up a one-hour sit down at the kitchen table appointment, which allowed me the opportunity to speak to both the husband and wife and listen and ask a few questions to see what their family situation, goals and needs were. Then I offered my solution.

After getting the "order," I would ask for permission to call and check in with them at least quarterly. And I would give them an estate planning guide with my card stapled to the back. In every case I asked for a referral after I closed the sale. I also assured them that I would check back with them if the future. I think at this point you can imagine that in addition to many other benefits of building relationships, asking and getting referrals will be a much easier for you because of the trust and sometimes the friendships you built.

Obtaining referrals, which is equally important to building relationships, will enable you to keep your prospect "pipeline" filled. When you realize the connection of trust and relationships, you can envision how the referral from a relationship who likes you and trusts you can turn what could have been a "cold call" into a "warm call." Needless to say, this will be extremely important for your sales success.

TAKE-AWAY NOTES
Chapter III

• The Basic Sales Process for any sales career: Attention/Opening, Probing/Listening to understand client's problems and needs.

• Then showing how the features of your products solve them.

• Finally getting the client to acknowledge the benefits of our product and commit to buy your product: Get the Order = the Close.

• I plan writing a supplement paper which will deal with referrals and post it on my website, *www.KeyPublishingCompany.com*

Chapter IV
Trust, Friendship and
Showing Up in Bad Times

In addition to his three reasons why people do business with you, my new manager also had us learn his facetious opening line: "Hi, I'm Jim Naughton; I'm your friend, it's the truth and I'm here to help you!" I say, facetious, because while some of my colleagues thought it was a questionable opening line, I believe I knew exactly what he was up to. He was giving us a "mind set," a way to be more than the competition. He didn't really believe any of us would actually say that upon introducing ourselves, but rather it was to always know that an important step in relationship building is getting your client to consider you as a trusted friend. You learned that my relationship with the New York advisor took about nine months to develop. While developing it, I want you to understand that I continued each day "showing up," which is what some of my clients, said was my best trait. I mean I showed up in the best times and also in a snow storm. I was dependable. I dressed in a conservative business suit with my shoes spit shined (I was a former Marine). We called this "PP," personal pride. Most of all, I made sure that I was always looked and acted professional. Some colleagues and some of the competition never quite understood its importance. It's all part of relationship building.

Remember the old saw, "a friend in need is a friend indeed." It's a quick way of saying that anyone can claim to be a friend. However when someone has a crisis, do their friends show up to lend a hand? It's when you really find out who the real friends are. It's the same in sales. There are a lot of products and a lot of salesmen out there. Will they go into hiding if something malfunctions with one of their firms products? Will you?

If you are working with me, you will call and visit your clients ASAP if there is a major product malfunction. You will have other products to sell, and if you had earned the client's trust and if they are a true relationship, they will buy from you again. Worst case scenario, if your products implode in a catastrophic manner and your firm is severely damaged because of it, in the unlikely event you have to work for another company in your industry, unless you move cross country, you most likely will be in a similar territory selling to your old clients. Do you think you might have a better chance selling to them, if you were there when something went wrong and you held their hand even while taking a little bit of abuse? "No question; yes you would."

If you are just beginning your sales career, upon reading this section you are privately saying to yourself, "there is no doubt, I know I would be there." Believe me, when I tell you that, during my forty years in sales, I watched some salesmen who never really built much of a relationship with any of their clients disappear in a crisis, whether it was a problem with a pacemaker or a mutual fund: Great for guys like me and you, because we would be there no matter what.

If it were one of my products that blew up, I would be on the phone and in a client's office "taking it on the chin" as fast as I could get there.

TAKE-AWAY NOTES
Chapter IV

• Build relationships, and become FRIENDS with them through TRUST.

• SHOW UP, especially in tough times, so they can count on you.

• Know that relationships take TIME TO BUILD.

• Dress for SUCCESS!

Chapter V
Empathy, Sincerity, and Service

You have just made a very nice sale to a new customer. It makes sense that you would want to obtain repeat sales in the future. You begin the process by telling the customer that you will check in by phone to see how everything is going, then you do it. If your organization allows for it, you have also mentioned that your in-house partner (maybe called a sales desk rep) will be calling to introduce him or herself and to be of future service along with yourself. YOU, make sure that this has been done. Again, you got your first sale. "Do you want opportunities to get more sales?" SERVICE, SERVICE, SERVICE!! I can't emphasize enough the importance of providing good service as a way to build and maintain great relationships.

My inside sales staff all had to have vast product knowledge before they came to work for me. This was a given. I mandated the following: Return calls yesterday and let me know of any major issues. Make proactive calls to clients as often as monthly depending on the client. I generally gave them lists of specific clients to call or not to call (meaning not everyone wants to be called and some only infrequently), and help me to solidify relationships, and to continuously to build their trust in me.

This was in ADDITION to the many calls that I personally made each day.

Not all your customers are going to be your friend, in fact, at the risk of vacillating from some of the information already provided, some potential clients can get turned off if you come on too strong in this regard. So, yes, it would be great to have many of your relationships become your friend, however, from a client's (someone who you made a sale to) perspective, they first and foremost have needs and problems they want your help with. Depending on your professionalism and the service which you provide, they might become a relationship and friend, but in my experience, some that I thought might turn into friends, just didn't.

Just like my first neighbor in our present neighborhood, he was a decent neighbor — he kept his property immaculate, we waved when we encountered one another — but if we got together at each other's home once every 2 years, that would be a lot. Our current neighbor is more of a friend. We visit each other often and get together for dinner usually once every couple of months. It's not easily explained: in my view it's a form of chemistry between people that exists or doesn't. However, if there is even a little of this chemistry existing, doing what I discussed so far will positively bring it to the forefront. Both neighbors keep (kept) their homes looking great which is good for the neighborhood resale value. Being good "friends" with the present neighbors is the icing on the cake. Customers can become relationships and friends which will enable you to become the best salesperson in your organization. If they don't want to become your friend and just continue to buy your products — that's the next best thing.

You have read that Relationship building takes time, as the saying goes: "Control the things that you can control and have the ability to realize and let go of the things you can't." Meaning that you take a customer you have recently made a sale to, then you and your team, SERVICE him/her the best that you can. This, combined with my earlier-mentioned suggestions, should provide you with a relationship; if it does not, you tried your best — go on to the next one. Make sure you and your team, in addition to SERVICE, show them EMPATHY and SINCERITY, as they are so important in the sales process, particularly relationship building.

Most people can tell when someone is being sincere and has empathy for their situation. While I have always believed that most individuals could learn to sell, I am not 100% sure everyone can learn the empathy part of the sales process, although I have sometimes seen competition appear to be successful without it. Their success didn't last very long, however, confirming for me my belief that many of those that can't will end up being what I describe a little later on as a "Flash in the Pan."

After you gain a potential client's trust and can see that he/she likes you, I would suggest that you continue to learn more about your clients and their business, so you will be aware when you see an article, a trend or a new marketing idea that might be of use to them. I would email, mail or drop off in person a news item that might help his/ her business (in person would be my choice). You shouldn't always overtly try to sell something every time you call or visit with the client. Rather you are selling yourself subliminally by showing a SINCERE INTEREST IN THEIR BUSINESS.

As I pointed out regarding empathy, sincerity is also something that can't be pretended, at least not for long. It was easy for me, because I have always cared about others, whether in a sales situation or personally. For my top relationships (I would label them with an A, B, or C, with A being my most valued relationship), I would look for any information, statistics pertaining to, and reaffirms of, why they purchased one of my products. My consultative deep probing enabled me to learn how the information might help their particular business. I would run all of this information past my/your compliance department or management, depending on what industry you are selling in. Once approved, if I believed it would be helpful to them, I would hand deliver it to at least all of my A's. In my last career I sold financial products such as mutual funds to clients — Financial Advisors — who in turn sold them to their customers.

So, in addition to passing out important news items for their business, I would also (without jeopardizing another client's confidentiality) supply them with marketing/sales ideas for my products that I see clients and some of my colleagues are using, possibly in another state, or maybe a marketing idea that some of my own competitors are using with similar products to mine. Again, you want to continue to be endearing yourself to your relationships.

TAKE AWAY NOTES
Chapter V

- SERVICE, SERVICE, and SERVICE some more.

- Return calls yesterday.

- Learn to empathize and be sincere with your relationships.

- Organize – label your Relationships in order of importance.

- Look for information, articles anything that will help their business and personal lives.

- Remember that clients, relationships, first want their problems solved; thus want someone who can solve them.

- If your product can't help acknowledged it, continue to try to help them and you will eventually get a sale because you're honest.

- Honesty builds trust and trust builds relationships.

Chapter VI
How Marketing and Selling
Can Complement Each Other

As your sales and relationship building continue to expand, in my opinion, you should begin to wear two hats. Meaning that in addition to your sales hat, you should consider putting on a marketing hat. To a degree, the two are intertwined. As a salesperson you generally are given a market/territory to cover when you first begin. Makes sense, right? You don't want to be competing with other sales people in your firm. What about your future prospects, clients and relationships? Sure, they have existing markets, but what if you can bring them new markets along with your product(s)? If you were selling medical pain management devices to orthopedic doctors, and you call on some Internal Medicine physicians, and you discuss the success your current doctor clients are having with your product compared with the negatives of narcotic pain medication, you are now employing the use of marketing with selling.

When selling mutual funds in my last career. I decided to point out a new market for Mutual Funds in the mid-nineties for some financial advisor clients of mine. The period was pre-separate accounts (where money managers later put together accounts that resembled mutual funds for wealthy clients, but were individual security holdings that the client actually would own vs. the pooling of their money with other individuals which is typical of a mutual fund).

My marketing idea was to fill a large ticket void. In that era, $25 million was considered institutional and it was rare to see a retail (for the general public) mutual fund trade over one or two million dollars. So I put together an NAV Pricing program (NAV = "Net Asset Value": mutual fund lingo, which is close to no load, i.e., no upfront sales charge to a client at the million dollar sales level). This allowed us to go after the pseudo-institutional market from $1 to $25 million which I believed we — my advisor clients and I — were missing out on. I put together a slide show with actual sales examples (including clients like universities, churches, municipalities, and fraternal organizations) that ended up bringing millions of dollars in sales while the average regular mutual fund trade was $10,000. In addition, we were still able to give our client, the advisor, a decent commission, which we paid out of corporate profits vs. the clients investments.

Previously we all had to compete with the No- load Mutual Fund Companies such as Fidelity. Up until the early '90s, we continued to have a sales charge even at the million-dollar level. This program was a win-win for me and my firm. As you might suspect, the advisors who utilized this idea in their practice wanted to see me more often and looked forward to hearing more sales ideas from me. Of course the size of my sales increased into the millions. I would have done well just doing things the way they were done in the past, however, I broke industry records by putting on my marketing hat and thinking "outside the box." Marketing opportunities are always changing, you must watch for them. I believe that one can do a little "marketing" in almost any sales career whether you're in Medical Device, Pharmaceutical sales, IT sales and others.

TAKE-AWAY NOTES
Chapter VI

• Put on your marketing hat and help clients realize additional markets.

• Maybe point them to a market one of your associates found in another state—

• Or a market that the competition located where your product would be a better solution.

Chapter VII
Selling with Stories and Cementing Your Relationships
(plus: KISS)

I was often asked to speak/sell to groups of a particular client's customers. Telling a brief simple story, enabled a client and his customers to envision how my product could solve problems; story telling is a technique that's been used over the ages. In the early '80s, I was selling tax deferred annuities with a high fixed rate. Because I wanted to instill the value of compounding interest rates on a tax deferred basis, I would ask the audience to envision Christopher Columbus landing in their town in 1492 and investing $1.00 at 5% simple interest. I would then ask, "What would it be worth in the early 80s?" Quickly answering it for them, I would reply, "That would be worth approximately $25.99." Then I would asked them to guess what it would be worth if Chris was able to invest it at 5% compound interest. No one would guess that it would be worth, excluding taxes, over $25 million dollars.

Sounds a little hokey today, but in the era it worked as a great sales tool. It allowed me to segue in and point out the salient features such as the tax deferred compounding provided by an annuity, to not only the advisor's customers, but to the advisor himself. I was continuing to make myself valuable to the advisor, my client. He would realize that I was important to his practice and would want to have me call on him often. My requirement, as you might guess, was for him to send me more business, and it usually worked. You can see how this relationship would grow and grow.

Later on in the 2000s, the Wall Street Journal and other major newspapers started providing us with statistics of the retiring Baby Boomer generation. One would often read "76 Million to Retire" as a part of the headlines, so I decided to put together another brief story to incorporate into my presentations. Using the Governments statistics, I would remind advisors and their older customers, that the time for accumulating assets was coming to an end, and it was time to think about distribution of their assets in a timely and efficient manner. On the chalk board I would write the two main concerns of this Baby Boom generation:

1. *They want a monthly check.*
2. *They do not want to run out of money.*

I would then offer to put together a personalized mutual fund hypothetical for them, showing monthly income based on their retirement accumulated assets. This is a feature of mutual funds known as a "Systematic Withdrawal," and it was always there, however, it was seldom used to sell a fund. Since the rules did not allow firms to forecast future earnings, I decided to use the decade of the '70s which was not a great era for the stock market, to help clients and their customers envision how this strategy could answer their two needs in the previous paragraph.

In fact, the market was at 860 in January 1970 and ended in '79 about 861 — obviously not a lot of growth. However, due to the fact that the stocks in a mutual fund, particularly in what we refer to as a total return fund (half stocks and half bonds), continued to pay dividends even in that lackluster market, we were able to pay out 5% a year even in the awful decade of the 70s from our total return fund and still have their principal intact at the end of a no-growth era!

Needless to say I was asked to present this simple idea all over New England to the hundreds of Baby Boomers who were retiring and their advisors. The idea brought in millions in sales.

Note: You will likely hear the following regarding your presentations as you progress, 'KISS,' i.e., "Keep it Simple Stupid." Incorporating a brief story or a parable could help you when presenting one-on-one or to large groups. A number of famous individuals have utilized them throughout history. In addition to telling a story, it enables the presenter to just plain talk to the audience, and along with throwing out a few simple questions, you begin to engage the audience. If you are new to public speaking, and if you can envision this method of presenting, it should alleviate some of your normal nervousness. Once you have mastered the art of presenting, you will have once more increased your value to your relationships. In addition, often other prospects will possibly hear of your new skill and want to meet with you, thus you have another way to build your sales pipeline. In my early years, I was staying at hotels all over the Northeast, so I would always check out the marquee in the hotel lobby to find a public presentation I could slip into. I would then watch other presenters and note what I liked and didn't like.

Can you envision the evolving of the building, the maintaining and "cementing" of my relationships? What else do you notice? You're correct if you said, "He's making himself VALUABLE to his relationships." I wanted them to view me as almost a partner, at least as an asset to their businesses. When I showed up, I wanted it to be an important and welcomed event. Subliminally, their minds are registering, "I can make money with his products and ideas." Because of the type of industry I worked in, I was often able to put on a lunch sales presentation to a large group.

My close in that situation was to get a show of hands as to who wanted me to stop by later and talk (sell) one on one. So when sales trainers would say to "always be closing," I heard "always be selling," and I was, meaning that I might, at lunch or in an office, provide some ideas, product features, and usage, then I would wait to attempt a close on my product until I got in the advisor's office. In the beginning of my book, I explained that I would discuss those things that worked for me, and proved to be successful. You will no doubt read other books on your selling craft and decide what works best for you.

TAKE-AWAY NOTES
Chapter VII

• Try to employ the use of stories, especially when selling to a group. Storytelling is a sales method used over the ages.

• Remember the KISS principle.

• Make yourself valuable to your clients.

• Always be selling.

Chapter VIII
Competition

In my book *Jump In and Start Swimming*, I discussed the matter of "How did I handle the competition?" The answer is: I didn't. I made sure I was knowledgeable of their products and their weaknesses, so when a client asked about a competitor or competitor's product, I was always respectful. And, with practice, I learned the ability to turn a client's question back to what my products features could do for them. I THOUGHT THAT GIVING ANY TIME TO THE COMPETITION WAS TOO MUCH. Also, I believe that outright bashing the competition diminishes your professionalism in the eyes of your prospects, clients and, yes, your best relationships. Don't do it! Fill their needs and solve their problems with your products. I also had a reputation of helping a competitor's salespeople when I could do so without giving them an edge over my products, and this in turn protected me from being trashed by the competition.

I plan on addressing this topic of competition with a future follow-up white paper on my website, *www.KeyPublishingCompany.com* .

TAKE-AWAY NOTES
Chapter VIII

• Learn the features of your competition's products, don't malign them.

• Use this knowledge to turn the conversation back around to "how the features of your product better fits their needs."

• Try not to give the competition any time.

Chapter IX
Some Thoughts on the Term "Flash in the Pan"

You might, during your sales career, hear the phrase "flash in the pan," which I briefly touched on a little earlier. This generally refers to a sales person who becomes an instant success starting out in sales. They happened to be at the right place and time. Their product practically sells itself, and the rookie sales person believes it was all about them. Then something happens, i.e., the product malfunctions, or becomes obsolete, and they have to sell another product. Nine times out of ten you never hear about these "one trick" sales wonders again. They just disappear.

A sales career can be very lucrative and fun, but it takes time to do things the right way; having a process of which building relationships is a part is the right way. Yes, you can do what I call "score" — take over a territory and strike gold for any number of reasons. It does happen, but a mature/seasoned salesperson knows his value and his contribution to the sales success. Yes, it's OK to bank the commissions, but it's also smart to stay disciplined and follow a proven sales process every day. Your manager might not agree with this saying, because of pressures, quotas etc., but sometimes the tortoise does beat the hare.

Having said that, I don't want you thinking you can take a laid-back approach to your selling career. I do want you to have faith in yourself and your products so that you can JUMP IN AND START SWIMMING: "Selling"!

TAKE-AWAY NOTES
Chapter IX

• If you happen to inherit a territory that explodes with sales early on, bank the commissions, but stay true to yourself.

• Continue practicing your sales skills, relationship building, consultative selling, referrals, etc.

Chapter X
Group Presentations, Seminars, Conventions

In many sales careers you will no doubt be asked to speak/present to groups from ten to 1,000, and larger.

In the Brief Overview (page 1), you learned how I grew a relationship with an advisor in New York in the early eighties with my sponsoring and presenting at his client and public seminars. Sometimes a lunch or breakfast would be provided; often we would have just coffee and cookies. In the early days I would open with a brief story that I thought the audience could relate to and would allow me to begin educating and selling my product. I would take a few minutes and relay to the audience some of the NEEDS of other groups I have spoken to. Then I would explain how my products were able to help those folks. Suggesting we (I and the advisor) could help this audience as well. My close was intended to encourage those interested to set up a personal meeting with the advisor whose assistant would be in attendance with his schedule and calendar.

Does this sound simple? It was. I wasn't a trained public speaker, in fact, the only previous presenting I had done was in and insurance classroom. I KNEW MY PRODUCT'S FEATURES and I saw how my product helped others, so in the early days, I would share this with the audience. Next, I asked them to envision how my product could help them while listing each feature (this was my way of utilizing ideas from trainers and books that say, "Tell 'em," then "Tell 'em again"); and that was it. This is another example of sales lingo, i.e., the "KISS" principle: *Keep It Simple, Sweetheart!* Including my opening story, I would finish in less than an hour. If I didn't know the answer to a question, I would just tell them that I would get back to their advisor within 24 hours with the answer. I often had a few slides to optimize the clients' understanding and which also served as an outline for my talk, so I didn't have to memorize the words which quickly became ingrained in my mind.

In the nineties, products got more complicated and I witnessed an evolution away from large group events to what became known as private client dinners. In this situation, the advisor would invite a few clients to lunch or dinner and instead of me presenting in front of them, we would have a conversation. This allowed me the opportunity to personally engage one on one with his clients and find out the needs of the invitees and begin filling/ closing them right at dinner.

In many sales careers you will be invited to speak at a corporate client's regional and possibly national conventions. In these situations you will be most likely describing your firm, your products and your role. If you're a rookie, you hopefully will be given talking points. You most likely would have made some presentations in your territory already and you probably will have some slides that you can also use as a type of talk outline. Telling you not to be nervous won't cut it; just know that most normal people regardless of their experience are always a bit nervous at the start of their speech. Maybe that's not enough consolation, but it is part of our human nature.

There are many books written on public speaking and it would make sense to read one. You can always join toastmasters or take a Dale Carnegie Public speaking course to sharpen your skills. Just so you know, while I mention my successes (and they were many), I was never considered the best public speaker. But, my production numbers made me one of the best salesmen, not only in my firm, but sometimes in the whole industry, and I shouldn't have to tell you what counted most to me and my firm. Imagine if I was also a great public speaker! So start practicing with friends, your girlfriend or spouse and try to become the best that you can. Just don't be too hard on yourself. I found that sometimes sitting alone and visualizing myself standing and presenting to a group was helpful. This also allowed my mind to create some ideas — clichés to sell myself and my product. A problem that I had to overcome, and it's common, was "dry mouth" from nerves. I practiced the timing of taking a swig of water that I made sure was handy at the podium. A trainer also taught me a trick to use in case water wasn't available. He said, "Start chewing on the sides of my tongue as if I had a piece of gum in my mouth." This act created saliva almost instantly! Not a perfect remedy, but even if someone thinks you're chewing gum, it's still better than not being able to form words with a dry mouth.

If you do get invited to a convention, in addition to schmoozing with your client(s), do some leg work with managers, meeting planning, etc., and see if you can get invited to an after-meeting cocktail hour with clients from your territory. I was once at a convention of 2000, and after the meeting, the Connecticut manager called my name out over the intercom and invited me to her private cocktail party. This is another example of what a relationship can do for you. Not only did all of my clients in her territory note my special invite, my firm's management did also. In addition to sales, getting a few "brownie points" is good for your career also.

TAKE-AWAY NOTES
Chapter X

• Practice your public presentations at home with friends and relatives.

• Take a speech course.

• Practice, practice, so that you get invited to speak at your clients' meetings and conventions. This will endear yourself to your relationships as they can use you and your speaking skills.

Author's Thoughts on Success:

The following ideas dawned on me over the years and I think that some of you might benefit from them:

In addition to the many success I have had, like many other aspiring salesmen and wholesalers, I also experienced some "soft" sales years. Sometimes, particularly in the beginning, it was my fault. Other times my products weren't competitive. Like the saying goes a "good farmer doesn't blame his tools." I kept my head down, kept working, and "showing up," trying to be at least in the top sales tier of my firms. I relentlessly followed the relationship steps outlined above and managed to build relationships by showing up, along with anything I could bring along to help clients, so when things turned around and my company and products got more competitive, I had things, i.e., "relationships," in place, ready for some quick sales, and that worked for me and will for you as well.

I have often been queried on the value of one having a good personality with regards to sales success. I think that that most would agree it is an asset. Having said that, I have witnessed colleagues and competitors who I thought didn't have a great personality become successful in spite of it. Some of them would make up for the lack of one by becoming more knowledgeable, consultative, more resilient and/or great golfer (which I never was). In other words, the successful ones found their way. Would I have been more successful if I was a better golfer? Yes, particularly in the financial industry. What I did was to co-sponsor tournaments and I made sure I sponsored a particular hole which allowed me to greet everyone in the tournament, all of whom were potential clients and relationships for me, vs. riding for eighteen holes for three or four hours with only three golfers. Then I would schmooze with everyone at the cocktail hour following the tournament.

So, yes, having an outgoing personality can be very appealing to clients, as well as being a scratch golfer; just keep in mind that the bottom line with relationship building is that clients have needs and problems that they want you to solve. Take care of those and everything else is "icing on the cake." If you don't, you're just going to drain your expense account.

For me, personally, I always looked for two specific characteristics in a potential sales trainee: Is he/she COACHABLE? I believed that if someone was coachable (WILLING TO LEARN FROM EXPERIENCE), I could teach them my methods for success. Everyone I ever worked for said, "I was coachable." In high school we had to write a paper on the topic: "Experience is a dear school, but fools will learn in no other. (Benjamin Franklin)." I never forgot it. Equally or even more significant is WORK ETHIC. My experience has shown me that any employee, particularly a prospective sales candidate, that has a great work ethic can succeed and eventually learn and/or overcome other prerequisites he/she might be "light on."

My other thoughts are about using your mind for success. As I was finishing college I happened to read a book titled *Pyscho-Cybernetics,* by Dr. Maxwell Maltz, a cosmetic surgeon, and his research on the power of the subconscious mind. A couple of his stories had a major impact on how I would begin achieving success with my mind and hard work. One was of a major dart throwing championship to be held in London. One of the two final contestants practiced throwing darts every day in a pub, while the other rented a small cottage in the Scottish Highlands. He hung large white sheet on a wall and would vision himself throwing bulls eyes on a dart board that he envisioned. He never threw a single dart. As hundreds watched, the contestant who only used his mind won.

The second story he shared was about an Army officer captured by the North Vietnamese during the Vietnam War and imprisoned for five years. A month after his release from a small prison cell he won a major golf tournament down South. When asked how this was possible without any practice, he replied, "I played a round of golf each day in my mind while in captivity, I envisioned the greens, the fairways, my teeing off, and my use of various clubs." I continued to become a student of the power of the mind over the years.

My suggestion to you is do not let your conscious thinking interfere with the attainment of your goals and your resulting success. If you have ever been on an ocean liner in the North Atlantic with a storm evolving, you have probably witnessed some mountainous waves. In the early '90s, I was on the QE2 with my family traveling from Southhampton, England, via the North Atlantic to New York, when we got hit twice by the same hurricane. Since I do not get seasick, I ended helping the ship's crew care for other passengers. I remember looking out of the glass doors at the stern of the ship and found to my amazement that I was actually looking up at the top of a wave we just rode down and I thought, "Mount Everest!" because it looked so huge.

Later in my sales career, while attending one of many conferences, I remember some motivational speaker asking, "What would happen if a ship could think?" Well considering my experience, my guess is that it would never leave port. Of course a ship can't think, but it does have a compass and it has a preplanned destination, or port (goal), which it will eventually reach, even if it's thrown off course by storms. We humans can do just about anything, and we learn something new every day. However, sometimes we just need to pause our mind and conscious thinking; take a breath and allow our higher divine power, that doesn't know, see, or fear the physical boundaries that our conscious mind sets for itself, and let it manifest our dreams and goals into reality. Spend some time visualizing in your mind's eye what you desire: more sales, abundance, prosperity and great health. It's not easy, our egos can be tough to handle, however, I found over the years that I needed to do this along with very hard work to attain my goals. I also have found it best to write down my long-term goals and my short-term goals separately for myself, and file them away to review periodically. (As a sales person you will most likely be required to submit your annual goals for sales management each year.) However, I always wanted to keep my personal goals private, knowing that how successful I was in achieving and surpassing my company goals would have a major impact on my personal ones.

Once I had written them down, I attempted to let my internal "compass," my subconscious, and my higher power steer me toward, and eventually reach, my goals. I say, "attempted," because it isn't always easy to get out of the way. I am not suggesting that you "don't think at all," just keep your mind and thoughts positive, and work as hard as you possibly can. Doing this is equivalent to taking a "leap of faith" as discussed in my self-help book *Jump In and Start Swimming*.

I always kept a picture above my desk of a duck on a small pond with the caption, "Act like a duck; calm, cool and collected on top, but paddling like a 'son of gun' underneath." You need to use some of your conscious thinking to stand guard at the entrance of your mind, and practice kicking out negative thoughts and/or turning them into positive ones. And remember, all the learning and training in the world cannot compete with "hard work," and "showing up." I have seen plenty of seemingly polished, great speaking and present-ing salespeople take a back seat to those who put their heads down, worked hard every day and knew they were going to be successful by con-tinuously trying and improving. They had faith in themselves.

You know your product, you know your com-petition's product, and you have practiced greeting a prospect with open ended questions during the sales process, along with probing, the importance of uncovering needs, and solving the prospect's problems. Closing will just take live practice in the field. That's it! Now begin to "act like a duck," and Jump In and Start Swimming — "selling." After a few sales, Relationship Building, Consultative Sell-ing, and Referrals will begin to resonate with you. As you begin employing these in your practice you will begin to exceed the goals you and your com-pany have set and soon you will be in the top 10% and eventually "Numero Uno."

Good luck and good selling!!

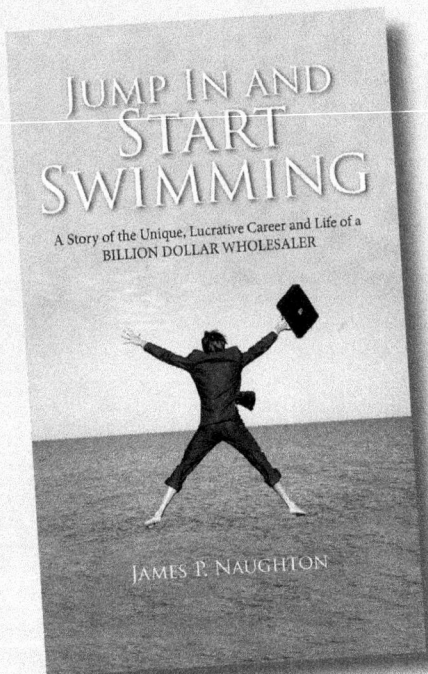

For purchasers of the paperback version of JUMP IN:

FREE Supplemental
College Job and Career Guide

CONTENTS INCLUDE: Applying for Jobs after College, Resumes & Cover Letters, The Interview, Contacting Companies, Suggestions for Getting a Job after Graduation, Consider the the Jobs Are, More thoughts on Websites, Resume Sample, Cover Letter Sample, Salaries for a variety of Careers)

No cost other than postage. US Postage cost = $1.50, International =$4.09** (based on one book.)
Mail a return address and a copy of your book purchase receipt, along with your postage check made payable to
JP NAUGHTON SALES PERFORMANCE COMPANY at:

James P. Naughton
51 Gosnold Road
North Kingstown, RI 02852

**Please email me for any questions you may have or if ordering more than one guide book for postage cost for US or other.
Email - *info@keypublishingcompany.com*

More information may be found at
http://keypublishingcompany.com/supplemental-guide.html
(ebook purchasers, please refer to the web page)

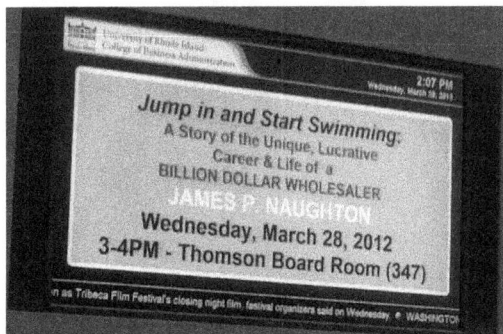

Also by James P. Naughton:

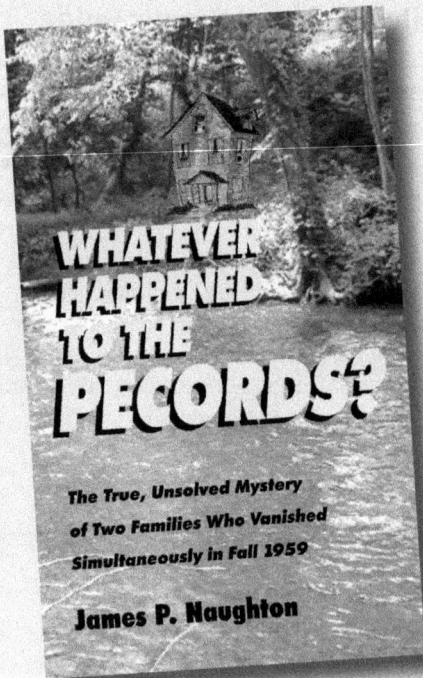

"A teenage true-life mystery story of a family that went missing. Food on the table, pots on the stove; gone forever as far as me and my buddies could tell in '59.

"Instead of calling the police, I called two buddies to do our own investigation and nearly got killed."

The author narrates a slide presentation on his book, *Whatever Happened to the Pecords?* (see opposite page) at Goodwin College, in East Hartford, Connecticut.

The college's location—before the college existed—figures prominently in the book, and Naughton acknowledges the kind help he received from the staff of the college when he was writing the autobiographical story.

𝔘𝔫𝔦𝔱𝔢𝔡 𝔖𝔱𝔞𝔱𝔢𝔰 𝔖𝔢𝔫𝔞𝔱𝔢
WASHINGTON, D.C. 20510

March 24, 1983

Dear Mr. Naughton:

Just a line to offer my congratulations on
your being named the 1982 "Man of the Year" and
your selection as Associate Vice President of
Dean Witter Reynolds, Incorporated.

This honor is, I am sure, well deserved
and is a fine tribute to your enthusiasm and
tremendously hard work.

With warm regards, renewed congratulations,
and all best wishes for continued success, I am

Sincerely,

Claiborne Pell

Mr. James P. Naughton
50 Arrow Lane
North Kingstown, Rhode Island 02852

This letter marks the beginning of a multitude of acknowledgements, awards, trophies and plaques that were presented to the author over the following 30-plus years (they are included in his book, *Jump In and Start Swimming*).